Kinl

MW01097081

DNA Wellness

Kinky Locs

DNA Wellness

Table of Contents

Introduction

Hello. I am deeply grateful that you have chosen this small booklet as a resource. As a licensed esthetician, wife, and mom, I was inspired to put this together in one place.

My daughter has thick curly hair like myself. As she got older and it got longer, doing her hair became a war zone. I saw myself in her. As a mommy, I knew there had to be a better way.

So many people are aware about the dangers in many foods and stay clear of putting toxic things in their body. Sadly, some do not realize what we put on our skin and in our hair is just as important. It takes on average 26 seconds for anything you put on your skin to be absorbed in your bloodstream.

_____

I struggled to find toxic-free products on the market for our hair type. Product after product was filled with ingredients like alcohol, mineral oil, polyethylene glycol, fragrance, and dyes. I mean why does my 8-year-old need to be using something that is also in antifreeze in her hair?

All recipes include Young Living® essential oils. They are the world leaders in essential oils and have been around for more than 20 years. Not all essential oils are created equal. For this reason, I do not recommend using any other brand with these recipes. To purchase essential oils get back with the person that handed you this booklet or you can check out our website at www.myyl.com/dnawellness.

From the bottom of my heart, again, I am truly thankful! Enjoy the journey and take good care of yourself!

Dayna M. Mott

Lady Day-DNA Wellness

_____

Kinky Locs

"The day I started loving people the way they received it instead of how I did, everything changed."

DNA Wellness

Dedication

This book is dedicated to my daughter, Aaylah, and anyone else that needs to hear these words. You are beautiful just the way you were created.

With tears streaming down her face she yells, "Mommy I can't wait until I am old enough to do my own hair!"

I quickly respond, "Aaylah, I can't wait either!"

"I'm going to straighten it like your hair and I won't have to deal with this anymore!"

This response took me off guard. "Why do you feel like you need to straighten your hair?"

"Because it will be easier. You never wear your hair curly. Look at all your pictures, it is always straight." Those words cut deep into my heart. The reality is I had no clue how to do either her hair, or my own. I had not equipped her with the tools she needed to embrace and love her natural hair. It was in that moment that I decided I was going to figure it out by starting with myself.

The recipes and information in this book is an accumulation of extensive research as well as a lot of trial and error. It is my hope that the information will be a blessing to those that read it! I am humbly grateful! From the bottom of my heart, thank you!

Disclaimer

This book is for educational purposes only. The information in this book has not been evaluated by the FDA. It is not intended to diagnose, treat, cure, or prevent any disease.

The publisher and author of this book cannot be held liable for any results you experience from the use of any of these recipes. Consult your physician with any medical concerns.

Ingredients to Avoid

Can we chat just for a second? We cover our mouth and nose when entering a toxic or germ infested environment. Sometimes we may even put on a mask. We avoid eating known toxins. When was the last time you drank bleach?

Here is the reality: the skin is not truly a protective barrier from toxin exposure. In fact, in some instances dermal absorption can be even more harmful than the other two. It does not have the filter of the nose or mouth. Neither does it have the filter of the digestive system. If you pick up this book and all you ever do is get rid of a few of these ingredients, I promise it will be worth your health.

Ingredients to Avoid

- Isopropyl Alcohol. Also used in antifreeze

- Mineral Oil. Coats the skin. Stops the skin from releasing toxins and can slow down normal cell development.

- PEG-Polythylene Glycol. Can contribute to stripping moisture, leaving the immune system vulnerable.

- Propylene Glycol (PG). Can break down protein structure. Also found in antifreeze.

- SodiumLauryl Sulfate (SLS) and Sodium Laureth Sulfate (SLES).Can cause damage to the immune system, separation of skin layers, rash, and inflammation.

- DEA (Diethanolamine), MEA (Momoethanolamine), and TEA (Triethanolamine).Common hormone disrupters.

- Parabens. Can cause irritation of the skin and disrupt the hormones.

These are just a few of the many ingredients to avoid. I challenge you to look at the ingredients in your personal care products. Flip over and read the labels. Take just one of those ingredients and type in your internet search bar, "the dangers of...." It will blow your mind!

Here is the thing. We cannot protect ourselves from everything, but we do have a measure of control within our own homes. A little poison here and there adds up. Ditch and switch.

Ingredients to Add

- Apple Cider Vinegar. Rich in vitamins and minerals good for the hair. Great for exfoliating.

- Aloe Vera Gel. Encourages hydration and locks in moisture.

- Vegetable Glycerin. Works well with other oils allowing deeper penetration.

- Marshmallow Root. Great for detangling hair.

- Avocado Oil. The Omega fatty acids bind moisture into hair follicles.

- Raw Honey. Natural humectant by retaining moisture.

- Flaxseed. High in Omega-3 fatty acids. Increases the hair elasticity which may lessen breakage.

- Jojoba Oil. One of the closest oils to a humans' natural sebum.

- Coconut Oil. Promotes a healthy scalp.
- Shea Butter. Great for binding hair follicles.

- Castor Oil. High in vitamin E, minerals, proteins, and omega-6 and 9. High ricnoleic acid makes it beneficial for hair and skin.

- Evening Primrose. Rich in Gamma linoleic acid. May reduce inflammation.

- Olive Oil. Great for strength and shine. Helps to protect keratin.

Ingredients to Add

Essential oils. This is just a short list of essential oils that can be added with the ingredients in the previous list to receive further health benefit.:

- Peppermint. Creates a cool, tingling sensation.

- Rosemary. Invigorating, woodsy stimulator.

- Manuka. Supports the appearance of healthy looking scalp and skin.

- Thyme. Stimulating, woodsy oil.

- Basil. Fresh, herbaceous stimulator.

- Lavendar. Fresh, floral oil.

- Sacred Sandalwood.™ Scalp support and clarifier.

- Frankincense. Healthy, youthful skin and scalp.

- Carrot Seed. Mildly sweet aroma with earthy, herbaceous notes.
- Clary Sage. Scalp stimulator.

- Orange. Encourages shine and protection of hair.

- Grapefruit. Encourages healthy blood circulation.

- Cypress. Encourages capillary strength and circulation.

- Cedarwood. Promotes healthy scalp and hair.

Kinky Locs

"When you walk every day with purpose, the best part of going to sleep at night is knowing that you get to wake up and do it all over again tomorrow."

DNA Wellness

Rinses

Rinses are a great substitute for a shampoo. Apple cider vinegar is the base for all the rinses in this book. Many shampoos and other hair products disrupt the natural pH level of our hair, which can dry out the cuticles of the hair and affect the condition of the scalp. To balance the natural oils in our hair we do rinses every other time we wash it.

My daughter and I have switched over to using rinses over the past year. Since then I've noticed that our hair has been better able to hold onto moisture and feels less dry.

Rinses

Relaxing Rinse

Ingredients:

- 2 cups Distilled Water
- ¼ cup Apple Cider Vinegar
- 3 drops Rosemary Essential Oil
- 3 drops Lavender Essential Oil

Directions:

Combine all ingredients and mix well. Section hair and apply directly to scalp. Let sit for 5 minutes then thoroughly rinse.

Note: You may combine ingredients in a glass spray bottle to spray on the scalp and store.

Rinses

Clarifying Rinse

Ingredients:

- 2 cups Distilled Water
- ¼ cup Apple Cider Vinegar
- 5 drops Thyme Essential Oil
- 3 drops of Basil Essential Oil

Directions:

Combine all ingredients and mix well. Section hair and apply directly to scalp. Let sit for 5 minutes then thoroughly rinse.

Note: You may combine ingredients in a glass spray bottle to spray on the scalp and store. This is my favorite rinse for a dry scalp.

Rinses

Sacred Scalp Rinse

Ingredients:

- 2 cups Distilled Water
- ¼ cup Apple Cider Vinegar
- 2 drops Sacred Sandalwood Essential Oil

Directions:

Combine all ingredients and mix well. Section hair and apply directly to scalp. Let sit for 5 minutes then thoroughly rinse.

Note: You may combine ingredients in a glass spray bottle to spray on the scalp and store.

Hair Masks

Hair masks are often used after the shampoo process, and sit on the hair to nurture the follicles. They may be used to nourish and treat tired hair. Hair masks typically will stay in longer, spending more time sinking in and absorbing into the hair. Between heat, styling, braiding, coloring, and environmental stresses the hair needs extra support.

I often use the Deep Moisturizing mask; it's one of my favorites! Between my constant use of relaxers, constant coloring, and flat ironing, my hair gradually lost its' strength and luster. This left my hair feeling and looking flat. Since incorporating this mask my hair now feels amazing and is growing like crazy!

Hair Masks

Hair Masks

Deep Rich Mask

Ingredients:

- 5 tbsp Coconut Oil (slightly warmed)
- 3 tbsp Aloe Vera Gel
- 3 drops Manuka Essential Oil
- 3 drops Carrot Seed Essential Oil

Directions:

Combine all ingredients and mix well until smooth. Section hair and apply from scalp to ends. Be sure to saturate the ends well. Let sit for 20 minutes then thoroughly rinse.

Note: Masks can be used instead of a conditioner for a deeper conditioning. Store the mask in an airtight container.

Hair Masks

Extra Moisture Rich Mask

Ingredients:

- 1 Soft Ripe Avocado
- 2 tbsp Olive Oil
- 3 drops Manuka Essential Oil
- 3 drops Frankincense Essential Oil

Directions:

Smash avocado until smooth. Combine all ingredients and mix well. Section hair and apply from scalp to ends. Be sure to saturate the ends well. Let sit for 20 minutes then thoroughly rinse.

Note: Masks can be used instead of a conditioner for a deeper conditioning. Discard any remainder mask.

Hair Masks

Power Protein Mask

Ingredients:

- ½ oz Plain Gelatin
- 1 cup Mineral Water
- 1 tsp Apple Cider Vinegar (ACV)
- 3 drops Carrot Seed Essential Oil
- 3 drops Clary Sage Essential Oil

Directions:

Mix gelatin and water until smooth. Let sit 10-15 minutes. Add ACV, carrot seed oil, and clary sage oil. Section hair and apply from scalp to ends. Be sure to saturate the ends well. Let sit for 20 minutes then thoroughly rinse.

Note: Masks can be used instead of a conditioner for a deeper conditioning. Store the mask in an airtight container.

Hair Masks

Honey Sweet Mask

Ingredients:

- ½ cup Honey (slightly warmed)
- ¼ cup Olive Oil
- 4 drops Rosemary Essential Oil
- 3 drops Orange Essential Oil

Directions:

Combine all ingredients and mix well. Section hair and apply from scalp to ends. Be sure to saturate the ends well. Let sit for 20 minutes then thoroughly rinse.

Note: Masks can be used instead of a conditioner for a deeper conditioning. Discard any remainder mask.

Detangling Spray

Detangling sprays have become our "go to" product when doing my daughters' hair. She has very curly hair, and a lot of it. For years we struggled to find something that would not bring her to tears every time she got her hair done. These detangling sprays were the solution. I'm sure she would agree that we are so grateful for them.

Detangling sprays have a water soluble base. When using them you will typically saturate the hair while still damp and comb through from root to end. It is very important that the entire shaft is saturated. Detangling sprays are one of the most crucial parts in styling. A good detangling spray makes the styling process easier and quicker. They may also be used to help prevent breakage.

Detangling Spray

Detangling Spray

No More Tears Detangling Spray

Ingredients:

- 8oz Distilled Water
- 2 tsp Aloe Vera Gel
- 1 tbsp Vegetable Glycerin
- 10 drops Grapefruit Essential Oil

Directions:

Combine all ingredients and mix well. Section hair and spray throughout the hair. Be sure to saturate well. Use a wide-tooth comb to comb through hair.

Note: You may combine ingredients in a glass spray bottle to spray on the hair and store.

Detangling Spray

Down to the Roots Detangling Spray

Ingredients:

- 1 ¼ cup Distilled Water
- ¼ cup Dried Marshmallow Root
- 1 tbsp Apple Cider Vinegar (ACV)
- ½ tbsp Avocado Oil
- 10 drops Grapefruit Essential Oil

Directions:

Place the marshmallow root in a pot with the water and heat for 15–30minutes on low until thickens and forms a gel. Stir constantly. When the mixture is thick as pancake batter turn off the heat and allow it to cool. Strain the gel and separate from the dried marshmallow root. Add ACV, avocado oil, and grapefruit oil. Section hair and spray throughout the hair. Be sure to saturate well. Use a wide-tooth comb to comb through hair.

Note: You may combine ingredients in a glass spray bottle to spray on the hair and store.

Treatments

The health of the hair starts at the roots. A healthy scalp can make the difference in healthy hair. Struggle with hair growth or loss? The scalp is an extension of the face. The scalps' skin is more delicate. It also has a higher number of hair follicles, sebaceous, and sweat glands. The problem is it has a lower barrier function, therefore making it imperative to have a scalp regime.

I've incorporated using treatments in my hair because for years I struggled with dry scalp. On top of that, I began to notice thin spots developing in my hair. I knew there had to be something that was missing that was causing these issues. Now I cannot tell you the last time I've had issues with dry scalp, and those thin spots in my hair are all but a memory now!

Treatments

Treatments

Scalp Stimulator

Ingredients:

- 1 tbsp Distilled Water
- 1 tsp Distilled Vodka
- 3 drops Rosemary Essential Oil
- 5 drops Lavender Essential Oil

Directions:

Combine all ingredients and mix well. Section hair and apply to the scalp. Massage into the scalp.

Note: Treatments can be used as needed for targeted support. Store the treatment in an airtight container.

Treatments

Long Locs Treament

Ingredients:

- 2oz Jojoba Oil
- 2oz Castor Oil
- 3 drops Cedarwood Essential Oil
- 5 drops Lavender Essential Oil
- 3 drops Clary Sage Essential Oil
- 3 drops Rosemary Essential Oil
- 3 drops Peppermint Essential Oil

Directions:

Combine all ingredients and mix well. Section hair and apply to the scalp. Massage into the scalp.

Note: Treatments can be used as needed for targeted support. Store the treatment in an airtight container.

Treatments

Overnight Moisture Treatment

Ingredients:

- 15 drops Jojoba Oil
- 15 drops Evening Primrose Oil
- 5 drops Carrot Seed Essential Oil
- 3 drops Cypress Essential Oil

Directions:

Combine all ingredients and mix well. Section hair and apply to the scalp. Massage into the scalp.

Note: Treatments can be used as needed for targeted support. Store the treatment in an airtight container.

Style

This is where you get to really let loose! This is the final step! Learning to style your hair will take time, practice, and patience. Experiment to find the look that is right for you. Gels are great for getting definition in your curl patterns, while the pomades will help to lie down and smooth the edges of your hair. One final rule to remember for this step: have fun!

Style

Curl Defining Styler

Ingredients:

- 8oz Lavender Mint Conditioner
- 5oz Distilled Water
- 3oz Aloe Vera Juice or Gel
- 2oz Coconut Oil (warmed)
- 3 drops Lavender Essential Oil

Directions:

Combine all ingredients and mix well. Section hair and apply from root to ends. Leave in and style.

Note: Store the remainder in an airtight container.

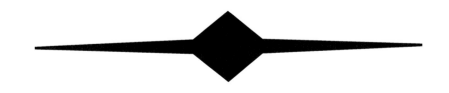

Style

Flax Seed Gel

Ingredients:

- 1 cup Distilled Water
- 2tbsp Flax Seeds
- 2oz Avocado Oil
- 2 drops Peppermint Essential Oil
- 3 drops Lavender Essential Oil
- 3 drops Cedarwood Essential Oil

Directions:

Bring water to a boil. Add the flax seeds. Decrease to medium heat and let cook for 10 minutes. Stir constantly. Strain all flax seeds out of the solution leaving the liquid. Refrigerate for 2 days. Add avocado oil and essential oils. Refrigerate for 3 more days. Stir and apply to hair. Style hair as desired.

Note: Store the remainder in an airtight container Keep leftover solution refrigerated for up to 2 weeks.

Style

Lay it Down Pomade

Ingredients:

- 2tbsp Beeswax
- 2tbsp Coconut Oil
- 2tsp Bentonite Clay
- 2tbsp Shea Butter
- 5 drops Lavender Essential Oil
- 7 drops Cedarwood Essential Oil

Directions:

Melt beeswax, coconut oil, clay, and shea butter on low-medium heat. Stir thoroughly. Remove from heat and add essential oils. Let cool until hardened. Style hair as desired.

Note: Store the remainder in an airtight container.

Style

Hold it Pomade

Ingredients:

- 2tbsp Beeswax
- 2tsp Jojoba Oil
- 2tsp Castor Oil
- 2tsp Avocado Oil
- 2tbsp Shea Butter
- 2 drops Lavender Essential Oil
- 2 drops Peppermint Essential Oil
- 2 drops Clary Sage Essential Oil

Directions:

Melt beeswax, jojoba oil, castor oil, avocado oil, and shea butter on low-medium heat. Stir thoroughly. Remove from heat and add essential oils. Let cool until hardened. Style hair as desired.

Note: Store the remainder in an airtight container.

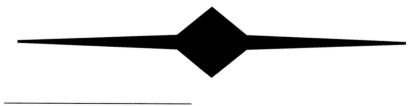

Kinky Locs

"I'm humble enough to know
I'm not better than anyone
and wise enough to know
I'm different from the rest."

DNA Wellness

Acknowledgements

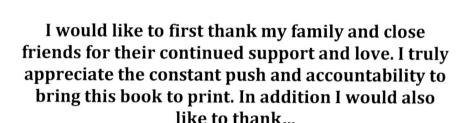

I would like to first thank my family and close friends for their continued support and love. I truly appreciate the constant push and accountability to bring this book to print. In addition I would also like to thank...

Nicholle Robertson, Writing Coach and Editor

Thank you for swooping in and making what seemed like a mountain into a mole hill. Your suggestions really helped me flesh out my book and for that I am truly grateful.

Anthony Mott, My loving husband

Thank you for being my number one fan. Pushing and encouraging me to stay consistent. I am so grateful for your patience and how you always challenge me to reach my highest potential.

Acknowledgements

Tashena Gozales , Sister

Thank you for holding me accountable to get this book finished and into the hands of so many people who have been asking about it.

Ronell Stokes, Brother

Thank you for never allowing me to be mediocre. And for always seeing the potential of who I am meant to be, even when I cannot always see it. It is refreshing to have at least one person that always gets me.

About the Author

Inspire. "I want to inspire people. I want someone to look at me and say because of you, I didn't give up."—Unknown

About the Author

Dayna is a wife, mom, licensed esthetician, and health enthusiast. Her associate in applied science triggered her interest in the human body and function. She has used this knowledge in her business and personal life.

In 2016, Dayna launched Lady Day, LLC. Lady Day, LLC., is a full health and wellness practice. She works tirelessly with clients and team members to reach their targeted wellness goals. She specializes in skincare, essential oils, pregnancy, child development, body function, diet, and self-care.

About the Author

Connect

Start your wellness journey with Young Living essential oils: www.myyl.com/dnawellness

Connect

Hey, hey everybody. We should hang out more than here in this book. Check us out on your favorite social media platform and let's get to know each other better!

YouTube: DNA Wellness

Podcast: DNA Wellness: Health Talk with The Mott's

Facebook: Dayna N Anthony Mott

Facebook Page: Ladydayllc-
https://www.facebook.com/LadDayLLC/

Instagram: YoungLadyDay1224

Email: LadyDayLLC@gmail.com

Kinky Locs

DNA Wellness

45050308R00031

Made in the USA
Lexington, KY
13 July 2019